Let's Talk More Often, Living with schizophrenia By, Amelia Victoria Andrews

Chapter1 Abnormal

This book is a true story. Norma is a 36 year old female and she will be 18 forever according to her. She looks like she's eighteen. Every where she go, she is carded. She will never understand how to function in society. Her body may change as times go by, but she wants to stay a teenager forever. Norma does not want to grow up and she refuse to. On Sundays Norma likes to go to Hot Topic to shop and listen to the music in the store. Norma lives like it is Halloween every day. Norma thinks there should only be three days in a week. Norma believes she has supernatural powers. Norma is also a spirit that can talk to other spirits and people who have died. She talks to people who have died in her family all the time. They help guide and direct her in this life. Norma has irregular heartbeats. Norma believes that she might not be human. Norma has visited other worlds through portals. Norma is fascinated with the afterlife. One of her favorite movie is Beatle Juice. Norma like the number three, her parents had three children. Norma uses three different clocks that tell different times all at once. Norma thinks that she is dead and sometimes she writes in red ink. On earth one month feels like a year to Norma. Norma likes fantasy. She also likes watching images on video games of dead people. Norma has intimate relationships with people that are not in this world. She also falls in love with people she never met. Her emotions are real. Norma feels like her real home is in another world and on another universe. She cannot relate to people on this planet.

Chapter2 Am I Dead or Alive?

Norma feels like no one can help her. She likes herself and feels misunderstood by people here on earth. Medications make her black out till she don't remember anything. She feels severely fatigue all the time. She does not trust anyone here on earth. People change and you never know how they're going to change. Norma thinks family is just here to help you get through life. Being on this planet make Norma feel like she's in prison. Norma escape is in music, dreams, and her dead friends. Norma drinks coffee, tea, and lemonade. She does not like a lot of the food here on earth that much. Norma jut eats to survive. Norma is confused about life. She doesn't understand why she has to live here on earth. Norma is not depressed. Norma is happier when she talks to other worldly beings that are not humans. Norma has studied new age but she does not like meditations.

Chapter3 Why Was I Chosen?

Norma did not like having a boyfriend. She thinks that you should be able to have sex with whoever you want without any obligations to him or her. Norma left all her relationships. She did not like being in a relationship. Norma doesn't want any kids. Norma doesn't have any kids. If she lived in a different world she might feel differently. Norma does not believe in love. Norma might get married if she was interested in what a man was offering. Norma needs complete freedom and open relationships. She couldn't just get involved with a man for all the wrong reasons. Norma's brother died and she doesn't understand why she had to stay on this planet without him.

Chapter4 Signs

Norma thinks she is visiting this planet to share what happens in her daily life. Norma likes the show Charmed. Norma does not like routines. Although she was born here on earth this world still seems foreign to her. Earth will never be Norma's home. She hated having to deal with bullies her whole life because they thought she was weird. Norma doesn't do drugs and people should not treat her bad like she does. Norma likes reading horoscopes. Norma is an Aries but she does not think that she is from the planet mars. Norma enjoys listening and reading songs and their lyrics. Music can occupy Norma's mind full time.

Chapter5 Am I Sleep or Awake?

Norma believes in God angles. Norma talks to people through books and social media. Norma talks to thoughts, television, and radio. I think Norma is listening now. Norma sleeps under a dream catcher. She likes listening to the sound of the ocean. Norma is a minister. She tries to find people like her but it is hard. She went to the library and researched abductions and ended up in paranormal. She listens to thoughts and she reads thoughts. Some day you will understand her in a new way. We are all still here with people who have died in many ways. The deceased leaves behind most of their objects. Dead people are in my thoughts all the time. Norma thinks that she is dead.

Chapter6 I Died

Norma thinks that she has kids in another world. If Norma had a boy or girl in this world she would name her kid God. Norma likes to read the words on tombstones. Norma's minister is a psychic. Norma use to go to a spiritualist church. Norma don't really cook, she prefers cereal, kettle corn, ice cream, or candy. I have to go see about Norma because her grandfather is having an operation. He is ninety years old in the hospital. Norma feels closer to angles than anyone else. Norma likes pumpkin apple scents. Norah Jones songs are playing in the background.

Chapter7 Life in Saturn or In Jail

Norma is approaching four oh and her social worker gave her a journal to write in. She doesn't seem to completely understand things. She believes that everything will come together so she doesn't worry. Sometimes people are in your live just for a second. Norma wants a statue of herself. People gets confused with things because some things are real, and other things are myths. You never know how things are going to turn out. Chapter 19, which is tomorrow, is a surprise! She feels that people might not understand her because she is not them. She loves her sleeping bags and skeleton headbands. She thinks she sees celebrities everywhere that she goes. You're never separated from art and spirituality according to Norma. She looks like a goddess in paintings and admires Madonna.

Chapter8 Notes

She wants to go to this intuition development class to sharpen her senses. She likes black and red roses and she is on many different dating websites. She likes when men help her without expecting anything in return. Norma volunteered at a law office. She spends her last pennies because she thinks today might be her last day on earth. Norma likes children's books. In every page you're in a new room. Norma has a question mark tattoo and red hair today. She likes the new tattoo rules in the military. What do you think of Norma? I think Norma is lost in the normal world. Norma's father works with computers and her mother is a hairstylist. Norma doesn't have animals. She believes that she was a mermaid and a fairy before. Norma wears black cat earrings and a raven necklace. Norma would read the horoscopes in the mental ill hospital.

Chapter9 Survive

Norma also has spider earrings. I am sharing Norma's life with you. She visits real hunted places and museums. She likes when people dress up in different eras and time travel. She doesn't like being around people much. Norma's brother likes swords, and now she wears one around her neck. Norma could never keep a job, her health failed her. There are billions of minds in this world. Norma will not have any grand children. Norma gets bored with going on dates. She thinks that men in books are cool. Norma believes that she is from another world that doesn't have animals. She likes her hair to be dark green today. This is a schizophrenia diary. She collects greeting cards.

Chapter10 Strangers

Norma has not been sleeping lately. Norma thinks that she is dead and that's why she's been sick. After Norma's brother died, she was given a brother in law. Norma is in love with ghost. Ghosts are as real to her, as you are reading this book. Once, she believed that she was married to the president of the United States. I think Norma's mom is her life saver. God bless the woman's soul. She thinks her uncle is Michael Jackson and prince is her cousin. She believes that she lives in this royal family. She just loves listening to lord. She eats walnuts, pecans, and cashews. She thinks living at home is like living in prison. I think she wish all this was true. She shouldn't be lying to herself. She believes nothing is what it seems.

Chapter11 Observations

Norma loves the pop culture. Norma' family stick together like a Jesus cross symbol. Her gray hair has turned into silver today. Norma's dad told her that every day is different and that things could get better. Norma's mom visits her in the hospital. Norma likes going to the library and book stores. In life there are many different sides to the same story. Everyone can form opinions and have views. Norma likes philosophy and she likes to explore things. She is very bored on earth. There are many beliefs and people tend to question things. Every day you start over new. Black is beautiful to Norma. Norma has been in the news paper three times for her good academics in school. Norma likes quotes. Norma also likes making posters, banners, cards, and book marks. Norma is talking to ghost right now. Can you hear them? She has a hard time understanding why a lot of people believe in God and they don't believe there are ghost.

Chapter12 Rich or Poor

Norma might change her name to pagan in the future. God gives us free will but designed us to be the person he created. We also create who we want to be. A psychic told Norma that she does not have schizophrenia. Norma doesn't have kids but she has a puppet. Norma believes that no one should be judged. We should be free to make our own choices. Everything happens for a reason. People who disagree with her, helps her become different. Norma struggles with relationships. Norma likes men but she doesn't think she will love them enough to stay with them. Norma believes that we are supposed to have differences. Norma only has social media friends and right now she prefers it this way. Norma believes that you can love who you want. When a relationship ends, you are no longer a match.

Chapter13 Thoughts

Her experience makes her a different person. She thinks she is like an alien visiting this planet. Sometimes she wants to be taken away from here. We live in a multidimensional world. Norma wants to learn a new language. Nothing is permanent. We are constantly moving. What is real to Norma may be different to someone else. Norma thinks she is from a new planet. New planets get discovered from time to time. Norma likes Monster High. Norma likes watching holograms. Norma believes that when you die, it's time to leave the world that your use to. Norma is very carefree. When she disagree with someone, she stills understands them. She believes that she has extra sense. Norma believes that she is saved because God forgives.

Chapter14 Distant

Norma loved her third grade teacher. She let Norma borrow her camera. Norma doesn't want to be an adult. She wants to be a grown teenager. There are many different answers to a question. For example, what are you going to be for Halloween? Norma wants to be someone who never existed before. She wants to be a book that talks. Be nothing but what I am is what Norma lives by. Norma believes that she was reincarnated into an art project. She also wants to be reincarnated into a necklace. Everything will eventually be turned into something. Norma watches people who have died on you tube like they are still alive today. In some ways they are. The legend still lives on. Norma believes that she is in wonderland with Alice.

Chapter15 Dreams

      After Norma's turtle and gold fish died she did not want to be around any more animals. Norma wanted a doll that looked like her. Norma don't believe that she' going to heaven or hell. She wants to go somewhere no one has been. Norma woke up when she heard the television say game over. One day Norma's roommate painted the house black and tried to kill her. She didn't understand why all this was happening. Norma was hit by a car while walking across the street. The person who hit her took her home afterwards.

Chapter16 Voices

Overall she is happy now. She believes that people on earth wants her dead because she is odd to them. She wants to keep Goth alive. Life takes on many different forms. Norma changes her hair like she changes clothes. She likes blue, black, and gold lipstick. Her fashion is always changing. Norma believes that she is needed here on earth right now, but there will come a time when she won't be needed. Norma believes that she will always exist even if she's dead. Norma will cross paths with many different kinds of people, living or dead. Norma doesn't think that anyone can harm her forever. Although she hears the devil speaks, she is not scared. Nothing was meant to last. Some images are destroyed. In Norma's mind, all dreams come alive. Norma does everything that she wants to in life. She doesn't know exactly why she's still here. Many people believe that earth is a school. Norma wants to move on to something that she is not familiar with. Norma wants to experience the unknown. Norma heard a voice tell her not to ignore her feelings. Search deep within yourself. Norma feelings give her a sense of direction, like a compass. No one is going to convince Norma that her life is a hallucination or a delusion, when some people think life is a game.

Chapter17 Therapy

Norma never had a drug or alcohol problem and she shouldn't be treated like she does. Sometimes Norma gets really bad headaches. Norma doesn't like seat belts but she wears them. Norma doesn't like needles. When Norma listens to music it helps her remember things. Norma doesn't like talking on the telephone. Norma has breathing problems. She is extremely fatigue. It's easier for Norma to talk to a women or children than a man. She has a hard time communicating and understanding men. People think that Norma talks to herself because they cannot see who she is talking to. Norma communicates with people all over the universe. She met an alien at a book store and online. Norma prefers not to talk to people on earth, she rather text them a message. Norma like concerts, taking walks, and watching you tube. Norma is not depressed.

Chapter18 Gifted

Norma thought that the president was coming to pick her up. When he did not show up, she went looking for him. She did not understand how it came to all of this. Norma fell in love with someone she never met before. Her emotions are real. She made him a birthday card and bought banana ice cream in lost Vegas. It was a love that she has never felt before. She would have done anything for him. She knew that he was married but she was ok with that. She did not want the responsibility that his wife has. She loved him and everything she knew about him. She thought that he loved her to. She bought a book about him and a picture of him. She really believed that they were in love. Norma had reoccurring dreams of their weddings. Over time she fell out of love with him. She started dating other people. The whole world knows who he is because he is popular. Life has a new meaning.

Chapter19 Tomorrow

Norma feels like she is trapped in some kind of a dream state. She thinks that tricks are being played. Norma loves her reflection in the mirror. Norma likes to spend her time reading. Norma only buys what she is naturally attracted to. Everyone with schizophrenia is unique. Maybe everything isn't a choice. Regardless, Norma has to be herself. Norma likes living a simply life. The past is gone. I trust that my life will be exactly what I want. I am discovering solutions. Today is my deadline. I am going forward.

Chapter20 Illusions

Norma worked hard in the private and public education school districts. Norma is happy with her accomplishments. Norma is looking forward to the future. She still wants to take trips and travel. She doesn't know where she will end up at. She doesn't know where she will be in five years from now. She lives like every day is her last. She lives with her family by the beach. Norma would love to live in another country. It's interesting how people change over the years. Some people change so much that you don't recognize them anymore. We all go through our own metamorphosis. We live with many different types of people. Some people are artificial, gay, transgender, psychic etc… There are also different religions. Norma sees herself as a tarot card. I find that life is very interesting. Every person lives in a different world according to what fits him or her personality.

Chapter21 Feelings

Norma's world is real and normal to her. She wants to be a teenager forever. Norma believes that people outside of this world communicates with us. They say music is the universal language. Norma communicates all the time, verbal and nonverbal. It's important to keep our minds open. Norma has irregular heartbeats. Norma receives important information from others. Norma is trying to understand human beings as well. We get answers from intelligent individuals. Some people might not think Norma is weird or crazy. Norma believes that she is sane but unique. Norma agrees more with psychics. Norma thinks we need more women ministers. Norma likes people who don't think she's weird or crazy. You can find a message in anything. Everyone in the universe is connected somehow. This is a puzzle internet. In time we will all understand what we need to. Everyone is a teacher. We can learn something from each other. Norma feels like she challenges herself. She looks for things that interest her. She is very interested in things outside of this world. She thinks outside the box and follows her heart. New things are waiting to be discovered.

Chapter22 Experiencing

When Norma looks back over her life, she feels like she is living in a year book. Pictures and words also help her remember events. Listening to music and writing is therapy. What is odd to you may be normal to someone else. Medication makes Norma dizzy. Sometimes she does not want to talk at all or she would rather talk with someone with schizophrenia. She wants people to understand her and treat her with respect. She wants to be able to relate with someone. She believes that individuals from other worlds help her more than people in this world. She would rather be with people from other worlds. Would you talk to someone from another world? Norma believes that she has to live this way to help humanity. She feels better when she talks to angles and people from other life forms. It helps her cope better on earth. She is sharing information.

Chapter23 Blurred

Norma doesn't think she is psychotic. She believes she thinks rational. Norma likes living in hotels not houses or hospitals. It is better for her to be around friendly people. She should never be locked up in a hospital. Some people have different experiences living with mental illness. The doctors just forced medication in her system with a shot. Now, she's unconscious again. When she wakes up she can't remember anything. She feels dizzy and woozy. She doesn't remember who her mom is or how she got here.

Chapter24 Church

Hi Norma, It's candy. I am a spirit board. Come talk to us. I've seen you before. You are psychic. Let's make magic. I've been casting spells on your latest technology. I believe you call it a computer. You lived on earth before. Ask me as many questions as you like. This is not a game. Everyone is dead here, weather you are a ghost or a human being. We are communicating, and you have angels who help you every day. You have a destiny to meet. Get ready for tomorrow and enjoy your opportunities. All of this is going to feel like a déjà vu tomorrow. Don't fool yourself, this is your fate. God listens to me. I am also everyone's friend to an extent. Always, trust in yourself.

Chapter25 Valentine's Day

Norma yelled no one is my friend. I only trust myself. I know angels help me. Every day I become stronger. Old songs are playing on the radio. We have endless weekends. I believe that I have alien babies living on other planets. I get really intimate with people who are not from this world. Art is at its best here. Life will never be the same. I am thirty six and it feels like I am eighteen. Horror seems to stay on. I am seeking something new. You can call me a fantasy if you choose. If you got to know me you would think that I am from another planet. I want the angels to take me to their home. Put my legend in a new bible verse. What if Goth was the norm? Life doesn't end here. It's not Halloween yet, but I lit an orange candle near a black cross today.

Chapter26 Funeral

You won't forget me. Somehow I will stay in your memory. I will also remain in things. I got the skeletons out of my closet. Everything s like an accessory, my perfume smells like the rain forest. Witches are painted on finger nails. It's hard to find purple straw brooms. Reflections are lost, I'm married to myself. I talks to my ancestors. I need to be in a free space spot, like I'm in a bingo game. I have a black cat that purrs in my ears. My hair is a new color almost every day. I celebrate Christmas, Halloween, Valentine's Day and birthdays 365 days a year. I like many different color fish nets and tights. I left my book of spell purse behind. Norma believes that she's Norman now.

www.ingramcontent.com/pod-product-compliance
Lightning Source LLC
Chambersburg PA
CBHW061949280526
45787CB00004B/1789